GW01157961

GTR MANCHESTER VOL I

Edited by Chris Hallam

First published in Great Britain in 2003 by
YOUNG WRITERS
Remus House,
Coltsfoot Drive,
Peterborough, PE2 9JX
Telephone (01733) 890066

SB ISBN 1 84460 282 6

FOREWORD

Young Writers was established in 1991 as a foundation for promoting the reading and writing of poetry amongst children and young adults. Today it continues this quest and proceeds to nurture and guide the writing talents of today's youth.

From this year's competition Young Writers is proud to present a showcase of the best poetic talent from across the UK. Each hand-picked poem has been carefully chosen from over 66,000 'Hullabaloo!' entries to be published in this, our eleventh primary school series.

This year in particular we have been wholeheartedly impressed with the quality of entries received. The thought, effort, imagination and hard work put into each poem impressed us all and once again the task of editing was a difficult but enjoyable experience.

We hope you are as pleased as we are with the final selection and that you and your family will continue to be entertained with *Hullabaloo! Gtr Manchester Vol I* for many years to come.

CONTENTS

Jordan Holmes	67
Natalie Wood	68
Ashlie Ball	69
Chloe Woodcock	70
Amy Schofield	71
Matthew Winstanley	72
Leshka Torskyj	73
Chloe Statham	74
Kyle Spinks	75
Georgia Knott	76
Toni Flynn	77
Daniel Knott	78
Ryan Morley	80
Jessica Gartside	81
Sarah Aspill	82
Iona Parry	83
Samuel Hayto	84
Jordan Reynolds	85
Victoria Trube	86
Zara Gibson	87
Abbie Stirrup	88
Laura Evans	89
Ben Pollard	90
Sarah Swinburn	91
James Hayden	92
Stephen Bowie	94
Liam Walsh	95
Katie Hogan	96
Leah Owen	97
Jack Cooper	98
Lewis Adderley	99
Jordan Cryne	100
Rebekah Bradley	101

Ringway Primary School

Declan Rowland	102
Craig Murray	103
Taryn Watts	104

Ryan Walker	105
Amii Whittaker	106
Sean Matthews	107
Gemma Cain	108
Haneefah Sheikh	109
Gage Abernethy	110
Jade Kelly	111
Emily Royle	112
Jason Moore	113

St Anne's RC Primary School

Carys Laing	114
Cameron Beedie	115
Adam Thompson	116
Joseph Dooley	117
Elizabeth Roberts	118
Megan Hathaway	119
Jade Healy	120
Olivia Dooley	121
Gaige Pendlebury	122
Serge Vernon	123
Abbie Tunnard	124
Jacob Smith	125
Rebecca Kakanskas	126
Daniel Butterfield	127
Clara Rogers	128
Callum Corneille	129
Jessica Ramplin	130
Rachel Cerra	131
Connor Doherty	132
Sruti Panda	133
Charlotte Conlan	134
Lee Costello	135
Greg Daniels	136
Anna Ward	137
Leanne Gill	138
Matthew Davies	139
Remi Owolabi	140

Jenny McDonnell	175
Katie Berry	176
Emma Summerfield	177
Elizabeth Summerfield	178
Jeannette Molloy	179
Cory Hallam	180
Faye Barcoe	181
Bryony Wilson	182
Emily Nuttall	183
Joshua Eccles	184
Ellen Corry	185
Catherine Corry	186
Jessica Walker	187
Amelia Payne	188
Kieran Coy	189
Shelby Teufel	190
Bethany Robinshaw	191
Sarah-Louise Doyle	192
Sophie Summerfield	193
Bethany Williams	194
Sean Coy	195
Alice Hibbert	196
Jennifer Williams	197
Michael McCullion	198

St John's Mosley Common CE Primary School, Worsley

Sean Pearce	199
Charlie Thompson	200
Daniel Mottershead	201
Sarah Hart	202
Zoë Gibson	203
Ashley Croker	204
William Hayes	206
Chelsea Renshaw	207
Sharelle Robinson	208
Shannon Tiernan	209
Michael Norbury	210
Daniel Winnard	211

The Poems

FREE AS A BIRD

I want to be as free as a bird
Although to you it may sound absurd
But right up they're within the clouds
It would be much better than it just sounds
Just imagine yourself, you can go where you like
Much more exhilarating than riding a bike
Over the rainbow I'd feel so tall
And with my freedom I would never fall
But I guess all of this is just in my mind
Because the freedom of a bird I will never ever find.

Leanne Hough (10)
Abbey Hey Primary School

MY MUM

My mum is sweet, like as a bird,
She has smelly feet, like a rhino
She's a good cook, just like a mother hen,
Reads books like a magic magician,
Smells like a red rose,
She sits for an hour watching soaps on TV like a
                                    staring monkey,
Her voice is a whistle of a bird,
She's got smooth skin like a feather from a pillow,
She's bouncy as a mattress.

Chelsea Hope (10)
Abbey Hey Primary School

MY FRIEND

She's as giggly as a hyena,
A chattery monkey,
Loyal as a lion,
A sackful of laughs,
A cheerful ray of sunshine,
Quiet as the dying sun,
Clever as an owl,
Pretty as a rose.

Jasmine Stewart (9)
Abbey Hey Primary School

THE NIGHT-TIME SPIRIT

The spirit of the night is hard to see
It sits behind you while you eat your tea.
It cries out loud in the night,
Moans and groans when dark turns to light.
It will haunt you anywhere
So watch out and be prepared.
You could turn the spirit into a cluster,
But you would have to be a ghostbuster.
When the spirit of the night has gone,
Watch out for the light of day has come.

Lauren Grantmyre (10)
Abbey Hey Primary School

AS WHITE AS SNOW

Snow is white
Snow is smooth
Snow is cotton around the room
Snow is like white wool on a sheet
That everyone would like to eat.
Snow is thick, as white as walls
Snow is like stars in the night sky.

Rebecca Bishop (9)
Abbey Hey Primary School

HAPPINESS

Happiness is a light colour,
Happiness smells like roses.
Happiness tastes like a bowl of grapes.
Happiness sounds like people cheering.
Happiness feels calm.
Happiness lives in your heart.

Hannah Paul (9)
Heaton Park Primary School

WAR AND CO-OPERATION

War is black, the gaping hole grasping
And pulling you into it.
It smells of fear,
Feels like darkness,
It lives in the heart of those supporting it,
And over all, tastes of pain and death.

Co-operation is the brightest yellow
It tastes of joy,
Sounds like bells ringing,
It lives in the brain,
And smells of sociability.
It feels like a warm blanket hugging the Earth.

Tomasz Kowalczyk (10)
Heaton Park Primary School

LOVE

Love is friendship
It smells like cherries
And it tastes like chicken
It sounds like happiness
It feels so, so, so soft
It lives in your heart.

Kieron Malik (10)
Heaton Park Primary School

FRUIT

F   abulous fruit so yummy and tasty,
R   umbling tummies waiting for fruit,
U   tterly, utterly, utterly,
I   ngredients of bananas, apples, grapes and pears,
T   ummies filled with fruit!

Abigail Grimmett (10)
Heaton Park Primary School

ANGER AND CALM

Anger is a screaming child,
Anger is a blood-red colour,
Anger smells of houses on fire,
Anger tastes sour, bitter and burnt,
Anger lives in the pit of a volcano,
Anger feels rough, burning and empty,
Anger results in a tight face with clenched teeth!

Calm is a relaxing lavender smell,
Calm sounds like the swishing motion of waves,
Calm is a deep, soothing blue,
Calm feels soft and spongy,
Calm lives deep down beneath the waves,
Calm tastes melted and soft,
Calm's effect reveals a smooth face with no worry lines!

Anoushka Brun (9)
Heaton Park Primary School

LOVE AND HATE

Love is pink,
Love smells flowery,
Love tastes like strawberries and cream,
Love sounds like a nightingale never-ending its song,
Love feels soft and gentle,
Love lives in a pink wonderland!
Love's result is a floating happy face!

Hate is black,
Hate is the smell of cigarette smoke
Hate sounds like a bell ringing in your ears
Hate feels like a fire burning in the pit of your stomach
Hate lives in your tongue preparing!
The result of hate is a hurt heart!

Emily Walsh (10)
Heaton Park Primary School

CLASS

C loakroom full of coats
L ook! There's the teacher
A t half past three home time
S omeone's being naughty
S top sit quietly!

Natasha Ilkin (10)
Heaton Park Primary School

DEATH

Down in your body you feel black,
It smells like a fireman's old boot,
It tastes like a sour lemon,
It sounds like screams down your ear,
It feels like a sharp nail hitting your finger,
It lives deep down in your heart.

Billy Sewell (10)
Heaton Park Primary School

HOLLY BERRY

H olly with its red shining berries
O ver the hills of the legendary Santa Claus
L ovely presents we open
L ittle candles burning brightly
Y ummy food that we eat.

B eautiful snow covering the ground
E verlasting evergreen showing up brightly
R udolph's mythical nose on pictures
R aisins and wine for grown-ups and children
Y ellow fires burning brightly.

Alex McIlgorm (9)
Heaton Park Primary School

ZARA

White and beautiful,
She belongs to me,
Cute and cuddly,
She belongs to me.

Galloping across the fields,
To try and reach me,
Swiftly walking across the fields,
To get to me.

She is my horse,
She is my Zara.
She is my best friend
She holds the key to my joy.

Most of the time we have lots of fun,
Even though I do not see a lot of her.
Her fur is so soft and so cuddly,
Often she rubs on me,
Really carefully, so she does not harm me.
Sometimes I sit with her in the field,
Even if it is cold.
Zara is my pretty horse,
Always gentle,
Really loving,
And I will adore her forever and ever!

Sophie-Ann Glynn (11)
Heaton Park Primary School

THE UNDERWATER WORLD!

Under the ocean waves there is a world,
A fantasy world of fish,
Octopuses propel themselves forward,
And some of them end on your dish.

There is a secret language,
That sea animals do talk,
It is a thing people don't understand,
When sharks start to stalk.

The seaweed sways in the current,
And clownfish hide in the corals,
This is the story of sealife,
And it does deliver morals.

Polly Rhind (10)
Heaton Park Primary School

I LIKE AND HATE

I like football
I like playing on my bike
I like Yugioh cards
These are the things I like.

I hate rugby
I hate having to wait
I hate my sister
These are the things I hate.

Jordan Hooper (10)
Heaton Park Primary School

I MAY NOT BE

I may not have the same skin colour as you.
I may not live in the same country as you.
I may not speak the same language as you.
But I *am* human the same as you!
So why all the war and fighting?
I ask you?

Charlotte Taylor (11)
Heaton Park Primary School

NATURE

N   ature is all around us,
A   lovely garden to run around in
T   rees swaying to and fro,
U   sing Mother Nature's touch,
R   abbits running in the forest,
E   xcellent things for us to see.

Kimberley Brough (10)
Heaton Park Primary School

PEACE

Why do we fight? Who made it right?
So what if we're black? So what if we're white?
Why do we have wars?
There's no good cause.
We shouldn't need a prison,
Because we should listen.

Everything should be fair,
People should care,
So stand in someone's shoes,
And see what it's like to have the blues.

Harriet Daniel (11)
Heaton Park Primary School

THE DUMP

I slowly creep in
It's dark, it's scary, it's smelly
I want to leave but still I venture on
I look around, my stomach rumbles on the floor
There's a poppadom.
It stinks in here,
It smells as bad as a skunk
I'm sure there's one in here . . .
Maybe on the top bunk
With the floor a wasteland.
An eyesore at that
If it weren't for me, I'd be a council tip, I'll bet.
Between the mist I see a door.
I decided to open it.
Oh no Mother's there! Quick move fast and take some cover!
I slid underneath all the rubble, not breathing only, waiting, waiting.
The door creaked open.
Please don't let me show.
'Louis come out and tidy your room'
I ignored her but oh no, I burst a balloon
'Now I've got yer!' she beamed.
I wanted to scream, tidying my room!
I'd rather be a Tudor and be beheaded!

Louis Szymanski (11)
Higher Lane Primary School

MY FRIEND

Talisa is my friend,
    we're friends till the end!
Talisa has short brown hair,
    hazel eyes and her skin is so fair.
Talisa is so active
    as a monkey.
    She is more caring and friendly
Than you would ever be.
    Why is she my friend?
'Cause she's funny and loopy
    and she's got such a trend!

Ffion Cook (11)
Higher Lane Primary School

THE BEDROOM JUNGLE

My mum says my bedroom's a tip but I say it's a jungle.
A cave of old smelly socks,
A trap made of clocks.
Vines of string,
Wild animals sleeping.
My mum tells me to put away my books but I say,
'No they're . . .
Leeches sucks,
And giraffe's favourite looks.
They can be fallen down trees,
For wild bees.
Or slimy snakes homes
And underground tombs.
But my bunk bed's for me,
So that's tidy.

Hannah Cherrington-Hall
Higher Lane Primary School

MY CAT

My cat is the best,
She's better than the rest.
Her purr is like a machine gun,
She loves being out in the sun.
Her claws are as sharp as a knife,
But she nearly lost a life,
When she ran away.
She stayed away, for more than a day,
But it was OK, I got her back,
The only thing was, she'd turned black!
In the end she was fine
I'm so glad she's mine.

Kirsti Thompson (11)
Higher Lane Primary School

MY FRIEND

My friend Faye has long blonde hair
      Dark brown eyes, and skin so fair.
Friends forever and ever and ever
      Put us together we're like two birds
      of a feather.
She's as lively as a bee
      Just you wait and see.
She makes me laugh
      And her jokes aren't naff.
She laughs like a hyena
      And sometimes scares the cleaner!
So why is she my friend?
      She's always very kind.
But can never quite make up her mind!
      She's always there when I need a friend.
Friends forever until the very end.

Amy Hughes (11)
Higher Lane Primary School

MCFC

MCFC is the best
They really do beat the rest.
United seemed to disappear
After they faced their biggest fear.
United were on the way to the League,
But City flew up to the top full of dreams.

In the second game we drew with Man U
We should have won, but we had a goal disallowed.
After that we felt very proud,
Keegan thought it was great.
But unfortunately Ferguson began to hate.

Daniel Muir (11)
Higher Lane Primary School

THERE'S SOMETHING OUT THERE

I walk across the bedroom,
Scared to death,
I know I must go on,
I see some clawmarks on my bed,
I'm glad I wasn't in it.
It would have took off my head.
I see some pawprints on the floor
It might be a lion.
I wish it wasn't a carnivore,
I stand on something as squishy as glue.

Okay then you guessed it, it's my dog, he's not a lion.
His real name is Brian.

Thomas Johnson (11)
Higher Lane Primary School

MY MUM

My mum
Has a big fat bum.
She wears a double D
She never needs a wee.
She comes down the stairs
In the funny clothes she wears,
But I love *her!*

My mum is really fat
She ate our cat.
I was really sad
I thought I was going mad.
She ate my brother,
As if she wasn't his mother
But I love *her!*

Hishem Khadhraoui (10)
Higher Lane Primary School

THE MONSOON IN MY ROOM

My room is a monsoon,
I see a monkey up a tree
It's my brother being as cheeky as can be.
I move on into my room,
Believe it or not it's still a monsoon.
It's like a forest,
But I still move on,
I find a door,
I open it up,
And I found my mum.
She shouts at me, I start to run,
I trip up and I start to cry.
A tiger attacks me,
It's my older brother.
I jump to cover
Then I see my little brother.
Oh no I've blown my cover,
My mum picks me up,
And locks me in my bed.
She said 'You just stay there,
I'll get your Ted . . .'

Jonathan Carr (10)
Higher Lane Primary School

JACK

There was once a boy called Jack,
Who truly loved to lack.
His handwriting was bad,
'It's a disgrace' said his dad.
He'd thieve and he'd pinch,
He'd steal pennies from Mr Finch.
At passing cars he'd throw some mud,
He even gave a heart attack to poor old Mrs Caffud.
But one day,
Jack stole some hay,
The horse saw him and began to chase,
It was as if it decided to race.
All of a sudden there was a mighty *crack!*
Then that was the end of Jack.

Daniel Moore (11)
Higher Lane Primary School

SCIENCE LAB

I enter my science lab
It's really my room.
Occasionally you hear an enormous *boom*
There is a car and a computer
As if its camouflaged like Jupiter.
My room is fifty yards long,
Rings of fire on my bedside table.
Hotter than hot from the Bunsen Burner.
My mum always yells
And she thinks it's a joke.
But one day she stopped laughing,
Because she saw smoke.
The joke *was on me!*

Luke Hooper (10)
Higher Lane Primary School

MY FAMILY

My family comes from another planet,
My mum's name is Janet.
My dad comes from Brazil,
And my brother's name is Bill.
   My family are so weird!

I really hate my brother,
I really don't need another.
My mum works at a bank,
And to be quite frank,
   It's sooooooo boring!

My dad is quite cool,
But he works at a *school!*
I'm so fab,
I'm never bad,
   I'm sooooooo cool. I *rule* the *school!*

Hannah Dixon (10)
Higher Lane Primary School

SCOTLAND

I stared over a valley, it's like a gaping mouth
waiting to be fed.
The mountains loom high like great giants
covered in heather.
The walls are like carpets of plant
I can smell the soil, the earth's favourite deodorant.
The wind howls like a distressed wolf
And the rain beats down on the ground
like a drum constantly being beaten.
This untamed land is a paradise, respect it, please.

Robert Pedley (10)
Higher Lane Primary School

SUNSHINE AT NIGHT

When it's hot, I have what?
I have sunshine in my pot,
I put it in the sea and it started to get bubbly!

A mermaid said, 'What is this?'
It's yellow, hot and bright.
It would sparkle in the night.

It would change colour, purple, blues and reds,
As we are sleeping in our beds.

Lucy Birchenough (7)
Highfield Primary School

COLOUR'S BLUE

Blue is the colour of my jumper
Blue is the colour of my shed
Blue is the colour of my eyes
Blue is the colour of many things
That's why I like blue.

Shaun Powell (10)
Manchester Road Primary School

NIGHT

Night is when stars are glowing bright
Night is when children are sleeping
Night is where you get together
Night is where you say, 'Everybody, goodnight.'

Rochelle Robertson (9)
Manchester Road Primary School

RED

Red is the colour of blood
Red is the colour of Red Riding's Hood
Red is the colour of my dad's shed
Red is the colour of my new bed
Red is the colour of my handwriting pen
Red is the colour of my brother's den
Red is the colour of a hot fire
Red is the colour of a painted tyre
All those things are red.

Sarah Newsham (10)
Manchester Road Primary School

BLUE

Blue is the colour of the deep blue sea
Blue is the colour of the bright blue sky
Blue is the colour of my new bed cover
Blue is the colour of my mum's blue car.

Blue is my favourite colour.

Katherine Bowcock (10)
Manchester Road Primary School

THE COLOURS I KNOW

Blue is the deep, the deep blue sea,
Blue is the colour that matters to me.
Pink a rose, and sometimes my cold nose.
Red, the colour of my bed,
Red is the hair on my head.
Green is the grass and the moss,
Green is the colour of my mother's horrid lip gloss.

Could anyone be more gross?

Rowanne Smalley (9)
Manchester Road Primary School

RED

Red is United's shirt
Red is a Ferrari
Red is the colour of my mask
Red is my pen
Red is the best
What is red?

Jason Metcalfe (9)
Manchester Road Primary School

LILAC

Lilac is the colour of my room
Lilac is the colour of a flower
Going to bloom.
Lilac is the colour of my favourite book
Lilac is the colour of make-up
Lilac is my favourite.

Colour!

Jennifer Madeley (9)
Manchester Road Primary School

GREEN

Green is the colour of grass
Green is the colour of leaves on a tree
Green is the colour of a flower stem
Green is the colour of my bed
Green is the colour of our table pot
Green is the colour of a mask on the wall
All of those things are green.

Jessica Hyde (10)
Manchester Road Primary School

BLUE

Blue is the colour of my school jumper,
Blue is the colour of City's shirt,
Blue is the colour of my bedspread,
Blue is the colour of my toy box,
Blue is the colour of my new pen,
Blue is the colour of my school ruler,
Blue is the colour of my extended writing book,
Blue is the colour of . . .

Craig Bradley (9)
Manchester Road Primary School

TEN HAPPY DOGS

Ten happy dogs licking wine
One fell over
And then there were nine.

Nine happy dogs putting on weight
One popped
And then there were eight.

Eight happy dogs going to Devon
One found a girlfriend
And then there were seven.

Seven happy dogs eating choc chips
One choked
And then there were six.

Six happy dogs learning to drive
One crashed the car
And then there were five.

Five happy dogs bashing their heads on the door
One got knocked out
And then there were four.

Four happy dogs drinking tea
One burnt himself
And then there were three.

Three happy dogs drinking out the loo
One got infected
And then there were two.

Two happy dogs playing with John
One laughed its head off
Then there was one.

One sad dog all on its own
He got bored and went home
Then there were none.

Jake Moroney (9)
Manchester Road Primary School

COLOURS

Green is the colour of grass,
Purple is the colour of fire,
Silver is the colour of money
that's stolen by a liar.

Gold is the colour of the sun,
Yellow is the colour of a lion's cubs,
Blue is the colour of the sky,
Brown is the colour of beer in pubs
and that's why I like colours

Holly Prescott (10)
Manchester Road Primary School

GREY

She has to know
where to go.
Attached by strings
attached by rings.
She wants to be free
this she cannot be.
Her life is grey
grey every day.

Her life is dull
everyone's is full.
She knows no one
she is lonesome.
These towers she climbs
further she cries
her life is grey
grey every day.

This path she walks
to nobody she talks.
Her life is grey, grey every day.

Helen Orme (10)
Manchester Road Primary School

COLOURS

Red is Man United, when they play at home.
Gold are the stars, all alone.
Green is the grass, swaying in the breeze.
Blue are my shorts, that go down to my knees.
Brown is the beer my dad has in pubs.
Yellow is a lion, protecting its cubs.
Silver is steel, glinting in the sun.
Grey is a spider's web, newly spun.

Michael Redman-Johnson (10)
Manchester Road Primary School

A Spell To Wake The Dead

Double double, this this, double double, that that
Double this, double that, double double, this that.
Eye of a human, bat's fang.
Skeleton of the dead to wake the Hell.
Fire burning as the cauldron bakes
And also half as a deadly snake.
Double double, this this, double double, that that.
Double this, double that, double double, this that.

Ryan Barrow (11)
Manchester Road Primary School

RED

Red is the colour of United's kit.
Red is the colour of football boots.
Red is the colour of a felt tip pen.
Red is the colour of a football.
Red is the colour of my friend's car.
Red is the colour of my United pyjamas.
Red is the colour of my United book.

Dion Baines (10)
Manchester Road Primary School

A Spell For You

A spell to make you invisible.
Put . . .
Ten terrible toenails from a tortoise.
Nine nasty nits.
Mix eight eels with an enormous elephant.
Add seven sickly snake heads with a silly sea horse.
Six smelly socks sucking a snake.
Five funny flying flamingos.
Add together four flaming fires flickering finely.
Three fantastic frogs added with a spice of flies.
Two terrible tomatoes.
One wicked witch.

Callum Bebbington (9)
Manchester Road Primary School

A Spell To Make Invisible!

Ten teachers trembling terrifically
Nine nervous nasty newts
Eight elephants eagerly entertaining
Seven slimy snakes slithering
Six shocking skunks smelling
Five frogs frowning friendly
Four frightened fieldmice farming
Three terrible terrifying toads
Two terrifying toads turning
One guess what?

Beth Deakin (9)
Manchester Road Primary School

A SPELL TO MAKE ME INVISIBLE

In my potion I will have . . .
Ten terrible termites from Transylvania
Nine nibbling newts knocking naughtily
Eight echoing electric eels eating hungrily
Seven silly seahorses sulking sadly
Six sick sea monkeys screaming angrily
Five flinging fishes jumping worriedly
Four flying flipflops flipping crazily
Three tiny toenails growing timidly
Two tickling tigers whiskers pointing sharply
One big witch cackling crazily.

Abigail Surridge (8)
Manchester Road Primary School

COLOURS

Red is the colour of a rose.
Orange is the colour of a setting sun.
Yellow is the colour of my hair.
Green is the colour of the grass.
Blue is the colour of the sea.
All these colours make a rainbow.

Alannah Stockton (10)
Manchester Road Primary School

MY FUTURE

What will be left for me when I grow up?
Will there be air to breathe?
Will the sea be clean?
Will tarmac cover the fields?
Will it stay green?
Will there be a sun to keep us warm?
Will there be a jungle for animals to live in?
Will the rivers flood the world?

Daniel Clegg (8)
Manchester Road Primary School

MY FUTURE

Will the stars still shine?
Will my mum still be alive?

Will my taxes go up?
Will there be enough water to drink?

Will Pierce Brosnan still be around to play James Bond?
Will children still go to school?

Will we still have Christmas?
Will we be close to doomsday?

Jordan Thompson (8)
Manchester Road Primary School

FUTURE

Will life change when I grow up?
Will litter cover all the streets?
Will dogs and bunnies still be alive?
Will elephants and rhinos survive?
Will pollution spread over the town?
Will rivers go right down?
Will people live on the moon?
Will there be an afternoon?
Will birds still fly?
Will people still be alive?

Lee Smith (8)
Manchester Road Primary School

MY FUTURE

Will life change when I grow up?
Will litter cover all the streets?
Will dogs and bunnies still survive?
Will rhinos still be alive?
Will pollution spread all over the town?
Will the rivers go right down?
Will people live on the moon?
Will there still be an afternoon?
Will there be new cars?
Will there be new made chocolate bars?
Will everybody drown?
Will there be a blue ground?

Jade Scrivner & Sean Bradley (8)
Manchester Road Primary School

MY FUTURE

Will the stars still shine in the moonlight?
Will there still be life on Earth?
Will bees still make honey for sweet a taste?
Will there still be water on Earth?
Will the sun still shine on Earth?
Will there still be animals?
Will there be air to breathe?

Christopher Walker (8)
Manchester Road Primary School

MY FUTURE

Will life change when I grow up?
Will litter cover all the streets?
Will dogs and bunnies still survive?
Will rhinos still be alive?
Will pollution spread over the town?
Will rivers go down?
Will people live on the moon?
Will there be an afternoon?
Will there be new made cars?
Will there still be chocolate bars?

Christie Marsh (8) & Keely Maher (9)
Manchester Road Primary School

In My Bedrooms

Ten little mice scuttling quickly
Nine fat elephants stomping loudly
Eight roaring lions running clumsily
Seven fat cats miaowing easily
Six little aliens scuttling proudly
Five little monkeys slithering slippery.
Four fat pigs oucking slowly
Three big fat hairy spiders creeping happily
Two snakes hissing happily
One boy in his cosy bed.

Charlotte Murphy (8) & Chelsea Allen (9)
Manchester Road Primary School

TEN HAPPY MEN

Ten happy men doing a crime,
one got caught and then there were nine.

Nine happy men eating off a plate,
one got smashed and then there were eight.

Eight happy men travelling to Devon,
one got lost and then there were seven.

Seven happy men who had big lips,
one popped and then there was six.

Six happy men all were alive,
one got stabbed and then there were five.

Five happy men needing a cure,
one found it and then there were four.

Four happy men all named Lee
one was called Jake and then there were three.

Three happy men have got flu,
one got cured and then there were two.

Two happy men lighting a bomb,
one exploded and then there was one.

One happy man pretending to be a hero,
he fell and then there were zero.

Sean Bradley (8)
Manchester Road Primary School

MY FUTURE

What will be left here for me when I grow up?
Will our family still be here to look after us?
Will there be daffodils to smell and roses for gifts?
Will there be decorations for Christmas time?
Will I still go to gymnastics and learn backflicks?
Will there be ducks in the lakes?
Will I still be here?

Jessica Murphy (8)
Manchester Road Primary School

AT THE BOTTOM OF THE OCEAN

At the bottom of the ocean I see . . .

Ten terrible turtles talking like a teacher
Nine naughty newts nibbling like a nit
Eight electric eels eating eclairs like an elephant
Seven silly seals swimming like a serpent
Six sarcastic sealions stalking like a snake
Five funny fat fish frolicking like a parrot
Four flat flounder fishing like a fox
Three thick tortoises tickling like a tiger
Two tropical terrapin tooting like a train
One worthless walrus walking like a wallaby.

Elizabeth Fenwick (9)
Manchester Road Primary School

THE SPELL TO MAKE ME FLY

Ten terrible toads from the swamp
Nine nasty nits
Eight evil eagles
Seven scary spook men
Six silly seals
Five fighting flies
Four flamethrowing fireballs
Three threaded thumbs
Two tangy termites
One orange octopus.

Michael Hall (9)
Manchester Road Primary School

AT THE TOP OF THE MOUNTAIN

At the top of the mountain I see . . .
Ten wicked, white, fluffy clouds that look like
chinks of wool.
Nine slithering snakes all slimy like slugs.
Eight elegant eels eating eclairs like elephants.
Seven silly seals squiggling like spaghetti.
Six slippery sea horses swimming stupidly amongst the sea.
Five frolicking ferrets fishing like a fisherman.
Four funny fishermen fishing quietly.
Three talking tigers tickling
Two tickly turtles talking terrifying.
One orange oak tree oozing with slime.
    No . . . can you guess what . . . ?

Amy Crowley (9)
Manchester Road Primary School

UNDER THE SEA

At the bottom of the ocean I see ten crazy crabs cracking crookedly.
Nine jumping jellyfish jumping like a jumbo jet.
Eight silly swordfish swimming slowly.
Seven snappy sharks snapping sillily.
Six stinky stonefish slapping smoothly
Five fierce fish fighting fiercely.
Four foolish fighting fish fooling around
Three horrid hooker fish hooking everything up.
Two magnificent moving fish moving fast
One shocking seahorse smelling badly.

Jordan Holmes (9)
Manchester Road Primary School

A Spell To Make Me Invisible

Ten nasty nits from New York
Add nine beautiful bears from Birmingham
Mixed together with eight enormous elephants from Egypt
Stirred in with seven dangerous dogs from Denmark
Adding six frightening flies from France
Poured with five juicy jellyfish from Japan
Jumped in with four terrible tigers from Tanzania
Pushed in with three terrifying toads from Turkey
Mix together with two terrible tarantulas from Canada
Poured in last part not least . . .

Natalie Wood (9)
Manchester Road Primary School

THE BOTTOM OF THE OCEAN

At the bottom of the ocean I see . . .
A slithery shark staring right at me
An ugly fat fish swam right by and looked at me
right in the eye
A daft dolphin waggled past supersonic real fast.

A crinkly crab crawled on the seabed, eyes so big
they filled his head.
An oily octopus with eight legs danced around
Whilst hanging his clothes with pegs.

All the shimmering shells hiding between the sand,
my they look so grand.
A huge hammerhead looking for food,
looks like he's in a real bad mood.

A slumbering sea horse wakes with a jump as a wet whale
hits the water with a massive thump.

Ashlie Ball (9)
Manchester Road Primary School

A Spell To Make Me Fly

Put in your cauldron . . .

Ten terrible toads from Thailand
Nine nasty nits mixed with spice
Eight enormous elephants mixed very nice
Seven silly seals dancing with
Six stupid eels
Five thin ferrets from France
Mixed with my delicate hands.
Four fishy fins mixed with a finger
Three pieces of glass to make it sharp
Mixed in with a golden harp.
Two terrible twigs with talking tails
And last of all
One juicy worm from the garden of snails.

Chloe Woodcock (9)
Manchester Road Primary School

MY FUTURE

What will be left,
for me
when I grow up?

Will there be pure
air to breathe?
Will flowers still sway in the morning wind?

Will air still sway?
Will birds still sing?
Will the grass still be trimmed?

Will dogs still bark?
Will cats still miaow?
Will I have one as my pet?

Will whales still blow water?
Will dolphins still sing their song?
Will fish still be caught in a net?

Will apples still grow on trees?
Will potatoes still grow underground?
Will crops grow in the fields?

Will milk still come from cows?
Meat, veg and fruit,
will they be good enough for meals?

When I grow up
and I'm in charge
what will it be worth?
If you have used
the goodness up
and destroyed the lovely earth.

Amy Schofield (8)
Manchester Road Primary School

A SPELL

Put in the cauldron . . .
Ten terrible toenails from a tortoise
Nine nasty nits
Eight enormous elephant ears
Seven silly snakes
Six squeaking birds from Barcelona
Five scary spiders
Four floating feathers
Three funny flying flamingos
Two stinking socks stinking badly
And one spell for you.

Matthew Winstanley (9)
Manchester Road Primary School

THE BOTTOM OF THE OCEAN

At the bottom of the ocean I see . . .
A jumping jellyfish jumping joyfully
A supersonic sea horse swimming super fast
An elegant eel electrocuting elegantly
A stinky sea snake smelling smooth
A ferocious fish flipping fiercely
A tremendous trout trying to talk
A curly catfish creeping cautiously
A trembling turtle trying to think
A creeping crab curling creepily
A snappy shark looking straight at me!

Leshka Torskyj (9)
Manchester Road Primary School

YELLOW

Yellow is the colour of some pretty flowers
Buttercups, daffodils in the summer showers
Yellow is the colour of corn growing high
Yellow is the colour of the sun in the sky
Yellow is the colour of the hot desert sand
Yellow is the colour of my mum's hair Mand.

Chloe Statham (10)
Manchester Road Primary School

COLOURS

Red is the colour of a flaming volcano
Gold is the colour of my fish Raino
Blue is the colour of a frozen pond
Black is the suit of James Bond
Green is the colour of lush grass
Bronze is the colour of a piece of brass
Yellow is the colour of the lovely sun
Orange is the colour of a baked ripe bun
Purple is the colour of a light violet
Silver is the colour of the buttons on a pilot.

Kyle Spinks (9)
Manchester Road Primary School

RED

Red is the colour of a lovely rose
Red is the colour of United's kit
Red is the colour of a warm fire
Red is the colour of horrible danger
Red is the colour of my brother's ball
Red is the colour of our library chairs
Red is the colour of a felt tip pen
Red is the colour of an exploding volcano
Red is the colour of my teacher's file
Red is the colour of a big loveheart
Red is the colour of a Woolworth's hat
Red is the colour of Bradleigh's car
Red is the colour of very bad anger.

Georgia Knott (9)
Manchester Road Primary School

GREEN

Green is the colour of grass
Green is the colour of a pear
Green is the colour of a bunch of grapes
Green is the colour of my bedroom.

Green is the colour of leaves
Green is the colour of our shed
Green is the colour of my bed
Green is the colour of my bike.

Green is the colour of my teacher's book
Green is the colour of a pound note
Green is the colour of a voucher
Green is my favourite colour.

Toni Flynn (10)
Manchester Road Primary School

HAPPY PEOPLE

Ten happy people working in a mine
One caught fire
And then there were nine!

Nine happy people putting on weight
One popped with a bang
And then there were eight!

Eight happy people going to Heaven
One went too far
And then there were seven!

Seven happy people chopping up sticks
One chopped his head off
And then there were six!

Six happy people feeling alive
One suddenly died
And then there were five!

Five happy people going on a tour
One got lost
And then there were four!

Four happy people sitting in a tree
One fell out
And then there were three!

Three happy people on the loo
One fell in
And then there were two!

Two happy people standing near Ron
Ron scared one off
And then there was one!

One lonely person sitting in the sun
One got too sunburnt
And then there were none!

Daniel Knott (11)
Manchester Road Primary School

ADJECTIVES

A happy clown, a worried frown.
A ginger cat, a hairy mat.
A bright sky, a flat pie.
A terrific pond, a tiny song.
A smooth foal, dusty coal.
Horrible mud, a horrendous flood.
A big hole, a messy pole.

Ryan Morley (10)
Manchester Road Primary School

COLOURS

Red is the colour of my new car,
Brown is the colour of my chocolate bar.

Yellow is the colour of beautiful soft sand,
Green is the colour of a rubber band.

White is the colour of my birthday cake,
Silver is the colour of my gardening rake.

Blue is the colour of the deep blue sea,
Pink is the colour of the face looking at me.

Grey is the colour of my oldest shirt,
Black is the colour of my new skirt.

Gold is the colour of my new ring,
Purple is the colour of the book I bring.

Jessica Gartside (11)
Manchester Road Primary School

POETRY

An adjective describes a noun
A silly clown, a worried frown
A furry cat, a terrible bat
A terrific hen, a magic pen
A big pig, a hairy wig
Horrible flu, a hot clue
A poor goal, a cold hole
A small bee, beautiful sea.

Sarah Aspill (11)
Manchester Road Primary School

COLOURS

Purple is the colour of my bin,
Red is the colour of my friend's grin,
Yellow is the colour of the sun,
Orange is the colour of the teddy I won.

Blue is the colour of the deep, deep sea,
Pink is the colour of me,
Green is the colour of the grass,
Clear is the colour of glass.

Brown is the colour of a chocolate log,
Black is the colour of my dog,
Grey is the colour of a dull sky,
White is the colour of snow on a mountain high.

Iona Parry (10)
Manchester Road Primary School

THE MAGICIAN

Today I'm a magician,
I'll do magic everywhere,
I'll do magic on the table,
I'll do magic on the stairs,
I'll do magic in the living room,
I'll do magic in the shed,
I'll wave my wand, till bedtime comes,
And then I'll do magic in bed.

Samuel Hayto (10)
Manchester Road Primary School

THE SLITHERING SNAKE

There it goes in the sand,
Slithering without a sound.
But watch out it might bite,
And easily beat you in a fight.
Its sharp fangs will go through leather,
It will go for your ankles because it's clever.
You think its skin is really rough,
Because snakes are really tough.
Don't worry with me on the job,
Oh by the way, my name is Bob.
The spitting cobra will aim for your eyes,
And surely blind you before it dies.
It will eat a gigantic bear,
Not a tidgy little pear.
It will eat things ten times its size
Not what we eat small pizza pies.

Jordan Reynolds (10)
Manchester Road Primary School

SEAL SONG

Around me, seas
Stretch endlessly;
Above me, sky.
A space to breathe,
A place to swim;
To pace the days
By moon or sun.
A place that time
Had kept from man;

No place to die.

Victoria Trube (10)
Manchester Road Primary School

SCHOOL'S FINISHED

School is boring, not a bit of fun,
Cold school dinners and one sticky bun
Hot in the playground, we still wear our coat,
Our teacher asks us where's our note,
Open the door school has finished,
Lessons haven't, *homework!*
Science, maths, English and French.

French is hard; I can't pronounce the words,
I can't be bothered doing it, I'll just sit and watch the birds,
Now it's teatime, fish, chips and peas.
I can't eat it properly as my cat jumps on my knees,
Science is quite easy; it is all about forces,
Haven't a lot of time, got to do courses,
English is all about poems,
Design and technology is all about sewing.

Zara Gibson (11)
Manchester Road Primary School

PLAYGROUND SOUNDS

We are the children in the playground
That sing and swing, sing and swing.

And we are the cats that
Purr and mur, purr and mur.

We are the children in the playground
That chatter and natter, chatter and natter.

And we are the cats that
Purr and mur, purr and mur.

We are the children in the playground
That shout and poul, shout and poul.

We are the cats that
Purr and mur, purr and mur.

We are the children in the playground
That cry and fly, cry and fly.

Abbie Stirrup (10)
Manchester Road Primary School

THE FUTURE

Will flowers still grow?
Will rivers still flow?

Will monkeys still climb trees?
Will dogs still get fleas?

Will people still have a cup of tea?
Will I still be me?

Will oil still spill in the seas?
Will children still eat peas?

Will there be running foxes?
Will people live in boxes?

Will people still run free?
What will my life be?

Will the grass still be green?
Will people still be mean?

Will snakes still hiss?
Will people still kiss?

Laura Evans (10)
Manchester Road Primary School

POETRY

A tiny home, a horrible dome,
A gorgeous cake, a frightening rake,
A terrible car, a beautiful star,
A fluffy mouse, a busy house,
A hairy clown, a messy town,
A happy bee, a horrendous sea.

Ben Pollard (10)
Manchester Road Primary School

FUTURE

What will the future store for us?
Electric pencils?
Rubbers that rub out for you?
Scissors that cut out for you?

Or will there be
Books that read to you?
Trainers that walk for you?
Rulers that draw lines by their self?

Will there be all this or
No seagulls in the sky?
No fish in the sea?
No trees in the forest?
All because no one cares.

Sarah Swinburn (10)
Manchester Road Primary School

LITTLE FOOTBALLERS

Ten little footballers running down the line
One fell over
And then there were nine!

Nine little footballers playing with weights
One broke his arm
And then there were eight!

Eight little footballers travelling to Devon
One went elsewhere
And then there were seven!

Seven little footballers eating pic 'n' mix
One got toothache
And then there were six!

Six little footballers learning to dive
One hurt his head
And then there were five!

Five little footballers going on a tour
One got lost
And then there were four!

Four little footballers climbing a tree
One fell down
And then there were three!

Three little footballers all got the flu
One had pneumonia
And then there were two!

Two little footballers looking at the sun
One got sunburnt
And then there was one!

One little footballer standing near Ron
One got too scared
And then there were none!

James Hayden (11)
Manchester Road Primary School

PLAYGROUND SOUNDS

We are the children in the playground
Crying and joking, crying and joking.

And we are the seagulls that
Swoop and dive, swoop and dive.

We are the children in the playground
Singing and chatting, singing and chatting.

And we are the seagulls that
Swoop and dive, swoop and dive.

We are the children in the playground
Kicking and kissing, kicking and kissing.

And we are the seagulls that
Swoop and dive, swoop and dive.

We are the children in the playground
Running and laughing, running and laughing.

Stephen Bowie (11)
Manchester Road Primary School

ALONE IN THE DARK

Help me, help me I can't see
This isn't the place for me.

Help me, help me it's really dark,
And it's really scary when I can hear that dog bark.

Help me, help me I can't sleep
I can't be bothered counting sheep.

Help me, help me I feel like I'm sleeping with the dead
And worse, I haven't been fed.

Help me, help me that smells really foul
I think it's that dead owl.

Help me, help me my bed's really hard
And my cover feels like card.

Help me, help me I want my dad
I'm really sad.

Help me, help me I'm going crazy
I can't move because I'm really lazy.

Help me, help me over there
That poster looks like it's getting closer.

Help me, help me it's not funny
That I need my mummy.

Shut up son!

Liam Walsh (11)
Manchester Road Primary School

I LOVE COLOURS

Peach is the colour of my nose,
Red is the colour of my rose,
I love colours.

Green is the colour of the grass,
Clear is the colour of my glass,
I love colours.

Blue is the colour of the sky,
Brown is the colour of my pie
I love colours.

Black is the colour of the night,
Yellow is the colour of my friend's light
I love colours.

Grey is the colour of my dad's shirt,
Purple is the colour of my mum's skirt,
I love colours.

Katie Hogan (11)
Manchester Road Primary School

SHE'S

She's funny,
She's clever,
She's beautiful,
She's young,
She's kind,
She's dangerous,
She's glamorous,
She's wonderful,
She's spectacular,
And she's cuddly,
That's why,
She's my *mum!*

Leah Owen (10)
Manchester Road Primary School

MONSTER

Black hair,
Like a bear.

Green teeth,
Like a leaf.

Big horns,
That look like thorns.

Yellow eyes,
That look like flies.

Long nose,
Like a hose.

Big feet,
Like chunks of meat.

Long nails,
Slimy as snails.

Big thumbs,
Like my mum's.

Looks sad,
Like my dad.

Jack Cooper (10)
Manchester Road Primary School

ILL WILL

Ill Will was always sick,
He always had a stomach ache.
He couldn't even give his food a lick,
You never see him with cake.

He hasn't been out because of his pain.
His friends want him to play,
But the doctor warned him about rain,
The poor lad might be better in May.

Will used to take a pill,
But that was no use.
They made him even more ill
Medicine is now his choice.

He is always at home
He has not for ages been in school.
He sometimes goes to the Dome,
He really thought it was cool.

Lewis Adderley (10)
Manchester Road Primary School

ADJECTIVES

A silly clown, a busy town
A steep hill, a long bill
A fluffy cat, a nasty rat
A cuddly cat, a spiky mat
Tired feet, a busty street
A wooden table, a tiny cradle.

Jordan Cryne (10)
Manchester Road Primary School

ALIEN!

Alien, alien,
Green spotty alien.

Alien, alien,
Tall fat alien.

Alien, alien,
Round plump alien.

Alien, alien,
Naughty silly alien.

Alien, alien,
Yucky, sticky alien.

Alien, alien,
Scary ugly alien.

Alien! Alien!

Rebekah Bradley (11)
Manchester Road Primary School

FOOTBALL MANIAC
(For Grandad and Cavan)

It was a cloudy day at Old Trafford
United v City.
United beat City
Oh what a pity.

'I knew they would have won,'
Said a fan called Joe Murr,
'It was luck!'
Said a man with a pint of beer.

'I'm off,' said Joe,
The man with a pint glass said, 'So am I,
See you at the next match.'
Joe said, 'I'm only going to get a pie!'

The next match they saw each other,
'How's your head?' said one.
'Killing me like mad.'
'I only went to get a won ton!'

Declan Rowland (11)
Ringway Primary School

THE PLAYGROUND

People running, people working
Teachers marking, teachers shout
Workers working, adults talking
Children get out.

Adults making, adults singing
Children playing, children messing,
People come, people go,
People are dressing.

Dustmen throwing, dustmen glowing
Children playing ping-pong
People read, people planting seeds
People's name called King Kong.

Craig Murray (10)
Ringway Primary School

OLD MEN AND WOMEN

They moan and whinge all the time,
They go on about city crime,
They have old things, and false teeth,
And put them in when they eat meat.

They ask for a 'cuppa' and a 'biccie' too,
'Biccie' is a biscuit and 'cuppa' is a brew,
How come they don't make the tea?
How come they only ask me?

I know I've been kind of bad,
And it turns out oldies are really mad,
So let's go on their team,
And let's stop saying they are mean.

They might be old but sure are cool,
(Even though some even drool!)
They give you cuddles and kisses too,
(But sometimes nearly swallow you!)

I love my nana, grandad too,
(Even if they look like goo)
They love me back and care a lot
(But out of their nose comes the snot!)

Taryn Watts (11)
Ringway Primary School

FOOTBALL DAZE

Playing on the football pitch
In the dirty ditches -
'United, United,'
All the girls will chant.

Playing against the best team ever
Never, never, never
You shall not win the cup
No way you'll win.

We beat them in time
And made them whine
We won the cup, hip, hip hooray
Never again shall they play.

United, United they rang for us
What a big buzz
Cos we're the best
Oh yes, oh yes, oh yes.

Playing on the football pitch
In the dirty ditches -
'United, United,'
All the girls will chant.

Ryan Walker (11)
Ringway Primary School

SUMMER'S SUN

Everyone likes summer
Jumping and swimming in the paddling pool.
Eating ice cream.
It is nice and cool.

The sun is scorching hot,
Everything is hot.
And everyone's smiling,
Dancing in one spot.

Dancing about
Eating lollies.
                    Summer is great!

Amii Whittaker (10)
Ringway Primary School

JABBERMOCKERY

(Inspired by the poem 'Jabberwocky')

'Twas Wednesday the naughty children
Did gyre and gimble in the PC room.
All mimsy was Miss Borogrove
And Mr Smith was gloom

'Beware the sweeper man, my friend
His broom that snarls, his chalk that catch!
Beware the headmaster bird, and shun
The evil Earring-snatch!'

His took his ballpoint pen in hand:
Long time the problem's end they sought -
So rested by the window
And sat a while in thought.

And as in toughish thought they sat
The sweeper man with eyes of flame
Came sweeping through the PC doors
And sweeping as he came.

They thought real fast as he went past;
The well-placed dust went smickersmack!
They left him stunned and with broom
They went galumphing back.

'And has thou got the broom, children?
Come to my desk,' beamed the teacher
'Oh frabjous day, caloo cahlay'
He chortled in his joy.

'Twas Wednesday and all the naughty girls,
Did gyre and gimble in the PC room,
All mimsy was Miss Borogrove,
And Mr Maths was gloom.

Sean Matthews (10)
Ringway Primary School

School Mockery

'Twas Friday and Jenny and Lizz did spelling with Mr Maths
And the children did spellings
When the teacher said them, they laughed.

'Twas nearly end of day and
Kids did English with Mrs English
With Mr English, Mrs English was tickling them
And they were ticklish.

'Twas end of day the kids were home
I was talking to kids
And they said they had a comb.

'Twas Friday and Jenny and Lizz did spelling with Mr Maths
And the children did spellings
When the teacher said them, they laughed.

Gemma Cain (10)
Ringway Primary School

AUTUMN

Down below I see children playing
Up above I see the trees swaying.
The lovely soft breeze
Is coming from the trees.

Everywhere I go, down every street
All I can hear is crunching under my feet.
Before summer was here, all great and warm
But now it's all cold and soon is the storm.

I miss summer, and so did my mother
But spring came and then went
Summer was here and now it's been left behind
So only autumn is on my mind.

Haneefah Sheikh (10)
Ringway Primary School

FOOTIE MAD

There's a footie team called the Skulls
They're completely mad
One called Peter
Two called Pad.

The captain Peter Pan
Lives in a van
While John's on the pitch
Having a can.

Andrew scoring hat-tricks
Joe has a patch
Training all day
Getting ready for the match.

There's a footie team called the Skulls
They're completely mad
One called Peter
Two called Pad.

Gage Abernethy (10)
Ringway Primary School

SCHOOLDAYS

We wake up early in the morning
All day we are yawning,
We were always on school on time
And some boys were doing a crime.

We are going to school
The small ones are playing with tools,
We are working hard
And my teacher called Miss Lard.

I was daydreaming in class
Hoping that I might pass,
I want to go home
And get a comb.

Now I am going to lunch
To chew and munch.
At playtime we get breadsticks
And I had a sweet mix.

Jade Kelly (10)
Ringway Primary School

WINTER

I look out at the snowy ground,
The trees are bare, there's not a sound
The ground is full of snow
The icy winds do blow.

Children playing in the snow,
Their rosy cheeks start to glow.
Children building snowmen,
Parents writing shopping list with a ball pen.

Children having snowball fights,
And the snow shines like lights.
Girls doing angels in the snow,
Children racing to their houses, 1, 2, 3, go.

Looking out the window at the trees,
While all the children are having their teas.
Children going to bed,
With sweet dreams in their heads.

Children are getting up in the morning,
Tired and yawning,
Going outside to play,
It is colder today.

Children having fun,
Eating their warm bun,
Pulling up their hats,
Hugging their furry cats.

Emily Royle (10)
Ringway Primary School

FOOTIE CRAZY

Shooting the ball in the net,
It was rainy and it was wet.
The sun came out,
I jumped about.

When I shouted, 'Hip, hip, hooray,'
I went to run a different way
I chipped the ball,
As I had a fall.

As it went flying in the air,
When it landed on a bear.
In the forest it landed,
As I came I was stranded.

I went to look for the ball
As I had another fall
I landed in a big black hole
As I saw a nasty mole.

It had dark brown fur
I looked at it as it was blur
I found the ball
After all.

Jason Moore (10)
Ringway Primary School

FIVE LITTLE MONKEYS

Five little monkeys jumping up and down
One fell off and banged on the door
And then there were four.

Four little monkeys jumping up and down
Along came a bee
And then there were three.

Three little monkeys were jumping up and down
Along came a girl 'boo'
And then there were two.

Two little monkeys jumping up and down
One jumped on a swan
And then there was one.

One little monkey jumping up and down
Then the sun shone
And then there were none.

Carys Laing (7)
St Anne's RC Primary School

ANTS

Five little ants sitting on the floor
One got stood on
And then there were four.

Four little ants sitting in a tree
One got sick
And then there were three.

Three little ants sitting in a shoe
One ran away
And then there were two.

Two little ants sitting on a swan
One went 'awat'
And then there was one.

One little ant all by itself
But it got stood on
And then there were none.

Cameron Beedie (8)
St Anne's RC Primary School

FIVE LITTLE CHILDREN

Five little children knocking on the door
One fell over
Then there were four.

Four little children in a tree
One was bad
Then there were three.

Three little children going to the shop
There was a tall man
Then there were two.

Two little children in a house
One was wet
And then there was one.

One little child in a treehouse
One was tall,
then there were none.

Adam Thompson (8)
St Anne's RC Primary School

FIVE LITTLE ORANGES

Five little oranges sitting on a door
One got eaten
And then there were four.

Four little oranges sitting in a tree
One fell off
And then there were three.

Three little oranges sitting in a shoe
One got squashed,
And then there were two.

Two little oranges sitting on a pond
One fell in
And then there was one.

One little orange acting like a hero
He fell out of the window
And then there was zero.

Joseph Dooley (7)
St Anne's RC Primary School

FIVE LITTLE SNOWMEN

Five little snowmen standing in a garden
One of them knocked on a door
And then there were four.

Four little snowmen standing in a garden
Along came a bee
And then there were three.

Three little snowmen standing in a garden
One of them said 'Boo'
And then there were two.

Two little snowmen standing in a garden
One threw a bomb
And then there was one.

One little snowman standing on his own
Along came a swan
And there were none.

Elizabeth Roberts (8)
St Anne's RC Primary School

FIVE LITTLE WITCHES

Five little witches sitting on the floor
One fell off the floor
Then there were four.

Four little witches sitting on the tree
One fell off the tree
Then there were three.

Three little witches building a coo-coo
One got stuck
And then there were two.

Two little witches sitting on a swan
One fell off the swan
And then there was one.

One little witch all alone
A vampire came down and bit her
And then there were none.

Megan Hathaway (7)
St Anne's RC Primary School

TEN LITTLE SHELLS

Ten little shells standing on a line
One fell off
And then there were nine.

Nine little shells standing on a gate
One fell off
And then there were eight.

Eight little shells waiting for their friend Devan
One didn't go
And then there were seven.

Seven little shells picking up some sticks
One didn't help
And then there were six.

Six little shells having lots of fun,
All six fell down a hole
And then there were none.

Jade Healy (8)
St Anne's RC Primary School

LITTLE CHILDREN

Ten little children standing next to a pine
The pine fell over
And then there were nine.

Nine little children a lion ate their mate
The lion went away
And then there were eight.

Eight little children flying up to Heaven
One fell down
And then there were seven.

Seven little children making chocolate mix
One fell over
And then there were six.

Six little children near a beehive
One got stung
And then there were five.

Five little children breaking the law
One got caught
And then there were four!

Olivia Dooley (8)
St Anne's RC Primary School

MY VILLAGE

Daffodils, roses swaying in the wind
Lots of cars racing round my village.
Clicking of lightning
Crashing and smashing and bashing
I hear flickering, it is the light bulb on and off.
I hear flickering, my cat purring under the gate.
I like cats,
I can hear my school friends in the school playground.

Gaige Pendlebury (8)
St Anne's RC Primary School

SILLY CHILDREN

Seven little children playing with ice mix
One fell in
And then there were six.

Six little children playing in a hive
One got stung
And then there were five.

Five little children going on a tour
One got left
And then there were four.

Four little children climbing a tree
One fell out
And then there were three.

Three little children trying to say 'boo'
One got scared
And then there were two.

Two little children playing on and on
One got dizzy
And then there was one.

One little child all alone,
He got bored
And then he went home.

Serge Vernon (8)
St Anne's RC Primary School

ON HOLIDAY

I am going to Torremolinos on Sunday 16th of February.
I'll be walking on the seaside.
'Wow!' everybody said
I'll be walking beside the crashing sea.
The sea will be swaying on my feet.
The sun will be bright and hot and orange.
It will be shining on my eyes
I will live in a hotel with a pool inside.
I will be swimming and will be happy all week long.

Abbie Tunnard (8)
St Anne's RC Primary School

The Sun

I like space, there's so much to learn.
Like if you go too close to the sun
Your eyes and ears will burn.
It turns hydrogen into helium
And this makes the light
Which is why when you look at it
You see it burning bright.

Of course you know the sun will die,
But you won't be scared and I'll tell you why.
It's lived for forty billion years,
And has another forty billion more.
Now you see there is no need to fear,
Because none of us will even be here.

Jacob Smith (7)
St Anne's RC Primary School

SCARED FEELINGS

I get scared feelings when I shiver.
I get scared feelings when my mum shouts.
I get scared feelings when I'm in a hurry.
I get scared feelings when I worry.
I get scared feelings when I hurt myself.

Rebecca Kakanskas (9)
St Anne's RC Primary School

THE ANIMAL FAMILY

The tiger lurks in the bushes,
While the deer pushes and rushes,
The tiger jumps out and has a bite,
While the deer gets a dreadful fright,
Now the deer knows how it feels,
To be one of the tiger's meals.

The birds know how it feels to fly,
They can see everything from the sky,
They can see animals run around,
Sprinting, jumping on the ground.
Birds can fly across the sea,
To find a place as warm as can be.

Whales are as big as big can be,
While they swim at the bottom of the sea,
Whales need to come up for air,
If not they would be in terrible despair.
Tourists come to see the whales,
With their gigantic, colossal tails.

Daniel Butterfield (8)
St Anne's RC Primary School

SUN AND MOON

I like to look at the sky at night,
To see the moon up so high.
To see the stars that shine so bright,
It shines in my room like a disco ball
All the way into the hall.

The sun is hot,
The sun is round.
The sun is so hot here on the ground.
The sun is as round as a pound
The sun is as bright as candlelight.

I love the moon and the sun,
Because they shine so bright day and night.

Clara Rogers (9)
St Anne's RC Primary School

THE SUN AND THE MOON

The sun is orange,
The moon is white,
The sun is so so bright
And the moon is so sparkly in the night.

The sun is hot,
The moon is not.
The sun is as round as a brand new pound
And the moon is shining all around.

Callum Corneille (9)
St Anne's RC Primary School

The Weather

The summer is hot,
The winter is cold,
Autumn is when the leaves unfold.

The sun is yellow,
The snow is white,
The leaves are golden brown
And all are a beautiful sight.

Jessica Ramplin (9)
St Anne's RC Primary School

THE SUN AND THE MOON

In the day the sun is bright.
At night when the moon comes out,
It goes around the sky like a disco ball,
It is as bright as the sun.

Rachel Cerra (8)
St Anne's RC Primary School

HAUNTED HOUSE

Drip, growl, bang, splat!
Blood, slime, potion.
Scream, shout, grind!
Skeletons, skulls, bones or
Dinosaurs,
Haunted! Haunted!

Scary, wary!
Sword, dagger!
Bats that flap,
And owls that hoot!

Connor Doherty (9)
St Anne's RC Primary School

SUN AND MOON

I like the sun, I like the moon.
The sun is so bright,
That I can't take the light.

The moon is shiny like a crystal glow,
With stars beside it,
Like dancing snow.

Sruti Panda (8)
St Anne's RC Primary School

CHARLOTTE CONLAN

C harlotte is her name
H ates carrots
A cts a drama queen
R ight handed
L oves sweets
O wns a Persian cat
T ea and cookies she utterly loves
T eamwork she uses
E ats lots of sugar.

C akes she thinks are yummy
O ranges she thinks are too juicy
N ickname is Charz
L oves licking lollies
A ctive
N ever wants to be unhappy.

Charlotte Conlan (9)
St Anne's RC Primary School

THE DIVER

One hot sunny day
I went to sea on my boat
I thought I would see a shipwreck
But
I saw something better
When I was down there
I saw goldfish and crabs,
But then I saw a shark.

So I just stayed still
It went past me
I set off again, I went past a bush
Then I came to a lot of gold
They all had a pattern on the pieces.

Lee Costello (9)
St Anne's RC Primary School

GREG DANIELS

G rateful is the thing I really am
R eally, really I don't like jam
E xcellent with his eating
G reg thinks teachers are rubbish at teaching.

D aniels is the name
A lways eats, I need to say again
N othing is rubbish apart from school
I   love swimming in the pool
E verybody likes songs apart from me
L ovely, lovely, is my tea
S o go away now this is the *end*.

Greg Daniels (10)
St Anne's RC Primary School

ANNA WARD

A   lways shows her stuff
N   eat and tidy at home
N   ice work when she tries
A   lways slow at working

W   orks quietly at school
A   lways kind to people
R   eads brilliantly at home
D   ances like a star.

Anna Ward (9)
St Anne's RC Primary School

THE SPOTTY DOG

Spotty dog
Black, white and vicious
It's like a cheetah running
It's got legs like a fox, that is cunning
I feel very tall because it is very small
The spotty dog
Runs around all day
Always wanting to play
He never stops for a rest
He always is a real pest
He never comes when I call his name
He is always busy playing a game.

Leanne Gill (10)
St Anne's RC Primary School

THE VEGETARIAN SHARK

I am a vegetarian shark
I gave up fish, I did
I've given up all biting
All I do is swim, swim.

I never ever sink my teeth
Into some fish's skin,
It only lets the blood rush out
And let's the dirty water rush in.

I once attacked a whale,
I swam straight at its head,
I woke up five days later,
In a ocean hospital bed.

Now I just eat seaweed,
It's tastier to eat,
Cos when I chew upon it,
It doesn't leave a foul taste like meat.

Matthew Davies (10)
St Anne's RC Primary School

SUNDAY QUESTIONS

Why is Sunday called Sunday?
Is it because it is the sun's birthday?
Is it because it is a sunny day?
Maybe it's because I like to play on a sunny day
Or maybe it's my son's birthday.
It's certainly not an ordinary day.

Remi Owolabi (8)
St Anne's RC Primary School

RAINBOWS

Rainbows in the sky
Rainbows over clouds
Rainbows over the fields
Rainbows everywhere
Rainbows painting sounds
Animals washed in colour
Animals appear in colour
Animals stay like that
Flowers very colourful
Flowers all alone
Flowers very happy
Flowers fully grown.

Krystina Selisny (7)
St Anne's RC Primary School

THE BEACH

The beach can be anything
Every time I come it's changed.
I close my eyes for a second and it's different
It's really, really strange.

The beach is such a huge place,
There's lots of things to do.
It fills my mind with lots of things
And there's water to swim in too.

The beach is relaxing,
You can be peaceful,
Or have your body flexing,
And do it cheerfully.

The beach is disgusting,
It's dirty and smelly.
There's lots of metal rusting,
I've seen on the telly.

The beach can be anything
Every time I come it's changed.
Go for a second and it's different
It's really, really strange.

Mikey Francis (10)
St Anne's RC Primary School

My Dog Cleo

Cleo is black and brown
She's always looking down
She is very nice
To be precise
But she can't come with me to town.

I love my dog
She comes with me for a jog.
She makes me feel happy
But sometimes she's snappy
So I just leave her alone.

Cleo reminds me of Sandy
Who wasn't very handy
She jumped around
And made a sound
And she always ate my candy.

Melissa Taylor (10)
St Anne's RC Primary School

A WATERFALL

A waterfall
The water runs down a hill fast,
Blue and bumpy.

It's like a racing car
It's also like a running bath
I feel tiny and cold around it
I feel as cold as an ice cube.

A waterfall
It makes me think of how much water
We have in the world.

Gemma Beedie (11)
St Anne's RC Primary School

MY BROTHER IS A MONSTER

My brother is a monster, cruel and mean,
Sharing his things he would never be seen.
He is huge and big and sometimes dotty,
So occasionally I call him Spotty.
He calls me a nasty, horrible name,
I tell him to stop but it's all the same.
He can be a bully that's why he plays tricks,
He knows the perfect time because his watch ticks.
When we argue he always growls,
His voice so loud it touches the clouds.
Sadly he frightens me very much,
But even though he's mean, he's still my brother
To the touch!

Kathryn Griffiths (11)
St Anne's RC Primary School

MY BROTHER

My brother is a giant and he is tall
He loves to kick his football at the wall.
He acts smart in front of his mate,
And that's something I really hate.
He always tries to fight with me
And the two of us can never agree.
At the end of the day he's my brother,
And I don't want any other!

Katie Hayward (10)
St Anne's RC Primary School

THE TURTLE

Down at the bottom of the big blue sea
I'm a jolly turtle and here's my plea.
'Help me! Help me! Help me out!
There is oil in my bubble.'
I scream and shout.
My mother, my father, my sister and me
Are slowly
    dying
    at
    the
    bottom
    of
    the
    sea.

Philip Douglas (10)
St Anne's RC Primary School

LION POEM

Lion, lion in a bush,
Move with caution,
You must hush,
It is almost ready to leap,
You must never move your feet.

Lion, lion jumps out bush
Change direction.
I must rush.
It is hanging on my tail
Must keep running
Will not fail.

Lion almost got me now,
I must live,
But don't know how.
I feel pain, I have not felt
Seems that I
Have not been helped.

William Green-Coogan (11)
St Anne's RC Primary School

EMOTIONS ARE FEELINGS

Sadness is a river,
It flows and does not stop.
It ends here at the bottom,
And shoots up at the top.

Happiness is the sun
It shines all day and night
It keeps you warm in winter,
And keeps on shining bright.

Anger is a thunderstorm,
It makes you feel so mad.
But in the end when you calm down,
You end up feeling sad.

Leanne Coppock (11)
St Anne's RC Primary School

CLOWNS

The happy clown bounces
into town
When he's wearing a stripy gown
He bounces in and out of stalls
Looks like he's going to a fancy dress ball.
He calls out to the children at the window above
Saying 'Come to the circus which you will love.'
The children follow him holding his hand
Playing instruments together as a band.
They skipped at the circus one by one
Excitedly awaiting, at last it has begun.

Emma Thompson (10)
St Anne's RC Primary School

MY MUM IS AN ANGEL

My mum is an angel
She is the best
Sometimes she needs a good rest.
She watches over me every day and every night
She will always be my light.
Her eyes shine like the stars in the sky
Sometimes they make me cry.
She smells beautiful every day
She will always be my angel anyway.
She is wonderful, she is kind
If I do something naughty she will never mind.
I love her because she's my mum.
When we play games they are always fun.
My mum.

Hollie McCaffery (11)
St Anne's RC Primary School

SADNESS IS A WILTING ROSE

Sadness is a wilting rose
Its brown petals drift away with each gush of wind.
Its beauty and smell are lost forever in the winter months.
The stem although tall and elegant is sharp and icy to the touch
The salty tears from the raining clouds fall
Silently, coating everything with clear droplets,
Each with a captured thought of sadness casting secrets
All around.
Standing alone, deserted and different from the rest
Sorrowful and sad is a wilting rose.

Danielle Baldwin (10)
St Anne's RC Primary School

MY CAT

My cat is stripy like a tiger,
Walking around the streets known as 'The Strider,'
Climbing through fences, running up trees,
Waiting to catch the mouse it sees.
Quick as a flash it catches its prey,
Just in time for the break of day.
Flies into the house as quick as a cheetah,
Only the humming sound of the heater,
Silently it sleeps dreaming of tonight.

Mark Duffield (11)
St John's CE Primary School, Middleton

FRIENDSHIP

Friends are people you can rely on,
Even when the times are rough.
They comfort you in every way,
That's what friends are for.

Friends help you when you are stuck,
Wherever you are they help you.
Even when it's sunny or raining,
That's what friends are for.

Friends aren't people who let you down,
They laugh about with you,
And have fun with you,
That's what friends are for.

Charlotte Black (10)
St John's CE Primary School, Middleton

FRIENDS

Friends are near
Friends are dear
Friends are ones we love to hear.

We love to laugh
We love to play
We love to have them come to stay.

Friends are neat
Friends are sweet
Friends are always good to keep.

They make me laugh and sometimes sad
But most of all
They make me glad.

Courtney Musgrave (8)
St John's CE Primary School, Middleton

MY HOBBY

Gymnastics is my sport,
But you have to concentrate really hard!
Even though you get a few injuries,
It is still really fun!
You soon learn your moves again,
Which is quite easy, if you remember how to!

For competitions, you can't be nervous,
Because you will do it all wrong!
It is a delight,
When you win all of the medals,
And your coach is surprised,
So everyone goes home with a smile!

Katie Holt (10)
St John's CE Primary School, Middleton

HORSES

H is for horses so beautiful and sleek.
O is for the oats they eat for their tea.
R is for riding over the hills.
S is for the saddle that you fit on with the girth.
E is for the horses eating out of their hay nets.
S is for the stables which I have to clean out.

A is for apples, which they love to eat.
R is for races, which I watch all day long.
E is for the enjoyment that I get out of riding.

F is for the fur that is lovely and soft.
U is for the uniform jodhpurs and boots.
N is for Nobby the name of my horse.

Sophie Hollingworth (10)
St John's CE Primary School, Middleton

MY BEDROOM

My bedroom, my bedroom is a tip
My mother says it's a skip.
Mother, oh Mother I say
This is my place
I like it this way.

My bedroom, my bedroom is all neat
My father says it's so sweet
Father, oh Father I say,
For what I say is -
I want it my way!

Jade Norbury (8)
St John's CE Primary School, Middleton

MY SISTER KATIE

K   is for eating KitKats
A   is for always playing with me
T   is for timing me on my bike
I   is for liking her
E   is for being everything to me.

Sam Stuttard (9)
St John's CE Primary School, Middleton

DRAGON IN THE GARDEN

I found a dragon in my garden
I fed it on grass and he drank water
I called it Joe
What more do you want to know?

Joe blew flames and would yell,
'Like to play a game?'
He puffed fire from his mouth
Steam from his ears
He smiled nicely and took away our fears.

It's time for Joe to go home
Which is a village outside of Rome.

Adam Dickinson (9)
St John's CE Primary School, Middleton

HOME

Home is where heat and warmth is,
Where the smell of a meal is,
With a gentle hand to tuck you into bed.

Home is soft and safe,
It keeps you out of trouble,
The cat and dog fight in-between my feet,
It gets me in a muddle.

Home is where you should be on a stormy night,
I hide under my covers because the storm gives me a fright.

When the storm is over all I like to do,
Is to watch TV.
Home is the best place in the world.

Holly Petrie (11)
St John's CE Primary School, Middleton

I USED TO HAVE THIS PROBLEM

I used to have this problem,
There's this girl in my class.

Whenever I see her my heart feels for her.
She's as pretty as a flower,
I wish I could just ask her out,
But when I try to she's always with a fella.

And her name was . . . !

Joshua Coleman (11)
St John's CE Primary School, Middleton

LINDA LEN WHO CHEWED HER PEN

Young Linda Len who chewed her pen
Thought it was cool for her boyfriend Ben
Then one day Linda felt funny
Her mum said, 'What's the matter honey?'
Linda didn't respond for she was a pen
And lost all her ink
That was the end of Linda Len.

Emily-Jade Newey (9)
St John Fisher's RC Primary School, Denton

THE WRITER OF THIS POEM
(Based on 'The Writer of This Poem' by Roger McGough)

The writer of this poem . . .
Is energy non stop
As strong as an anchor
As gentle as a dream
As fast as a hare
As slow as a turtle
As happy as a fluttering butterfly
As silly as a clown
As bold as a boxing glove
As cool as a skateboarder
As smooth as a silky quilt
As peaceful as the cold coming winter.

Chloe Hogan (9)
St John Fisher's RC Primary School, Denton

JENNY JEN CHEWS HER PEN

Jenny Jen chewed her pen at school
Her teacher thought she was a fool
She swallowed some ink one night
And she got a big fright
So ill in bed she did lay
And then Jenny Jen did pass away.

Grace Nolan (9)
St John Fisher's RC Primary School, Denton

THE WRITER OF THIS POEM
(Based on the 'Writer of This Poem' by Roger McGough)

The writer of this poem is . . .
As tall as a skyscraper
As strong as a wrestler
As gentle as a feather.

As fast as a bull
As slow as a slug
As happy as a birthday boy
As silly as a clown.

As scary as a monster
As busy as can be
As fat as a pig
As colourful as a rainbow.

Ryan Howard (9)
St John Fisher's RC Primary School, Denton

THE WRITER OF THIS POEM

(Based on 'The Writer of This Poem' By Roger McGough)

The writer of this poem . . .
Is a groovy groovy chick
As strong as a lion
As gentle as some silk.

As fast as a horse
As slow as a slug
As happy as a princess
As silly as a little elf.

As cheeky as a monkey
As cool as a lolly ice
As pretty as a rose
As clever as a witch.

Stephanie Underwood (8)
St John Fisher's RC Primary School, Denton

THE WRITER OF THIS POEM

(Based on 'The Writer of This Poem' by Roger McGough)

The writer of this poem . . .
Is as small as can be
As strong as a lioness
As gentle as a deer
As fast as a flash of lightning
As slow as a turtle
As happy as an elf
As soft as a rose petal
As hard as gold
As colourful as a rainbow
As soothing as a dream.

Sara McDonnell (8)
St John Fisher's RC Primary School, Denton

THE WRITER OF THIS POEM
(Based on 'The Writer of This Poem' by Roger McGough)

The writer of this poem . . .
Is as playful as a puppy
As strong as a muscle
As gentle as a deer.

As fast as a cheetah
As slow as a penguin
As happy as a smile
As silly as a clown.

As clever as a calculator
As loud as the Niagara Falls
As tricky as a calculator.

George Payne (8)
St John Fisher's RC Primary School, Denton

THE WRITER OF THIS POEM

(Based on 'The Writer of This Poem' by Roger McGough)

The writer of this poem . . .
Is as small as can be
As strong as a lioness
As gentle as a deer.

As fast as a flash of lightning
As slow as a turtle
As happy as an elf
As silly as a clown.

As soft as a rose petal
As hard as gold
As colourful as a rainbow
As soothing as a dream.

Hollie Tanker (8)
St John Fisher's RC Primary School, Denton

KAT JENN WHO CHEWS HER PEN

There was a young girl called Kat Jenn
The problem, she chewed a pen
Her friends said she looked a fool
But she thought she looked quite cool
So one night she went to bed
The very next day she was dead.

Chloe Hickinbotham (8)
St John Fisher's RC Primary School, Denton

THE WRITER OF THIS POEM
(Based on 'The Writer of This Poem' by Roger McGough)

The writer of this poem . . .
Is smaller than a tree
As strong as an angry bear
As gentle as a light breeze
As fast as a wound up turtle
As slow as a tortoise
As happy as a birthday boy
As silly as a hyperactive clown
As brave as a tiger
As vicious as a rhino
As smart as an elephant
As busy as a bee.

Ryan Heaney (8)
St John Fisher's RC Primary School, Denton

YOUNG LINDA LEN

I'll tell you a story of young Linda Len
Who had a bad habit of chewing a pen
The pen she was chewing was completely new
So don't start chewing your pen too
Later that day she died of poison and pain
Poor Linda Len was never seen again.

Amanda Simpson (8)
St John Fisher's RC Primary School, Denton

THE WRITER OF THIS POEM
(Based on 'The Writer of This Poem' by Roger McGough)

The writer of this poem . . .
Is a groovy chick
As strong as a lion
As gentle as a hamster.

As fast as a cheetah
As slow as a mouse
As happy as a birthday girl
As silly as a clown.

As funny as a monkey
As daring as a devil
As thin as a ruler
As clever as a cat
As pretty as a princess.

Alexandra Robinshaw (9)
St John Fisher's RC Primary School, Denton

THE WRITER OF THIS POEM
(Based on 'The Writer of This Poem' by Roger McGough)

The writer of this poem . . .
Is as cool as a skateboard
As strong as a lion
As gentle as a hamster

As fast as a cheetah
As slow as a turtle
As happy as a birthday girl
As silly as a clown.

As funky as a groovy chick
As daring as a devil
As thin as a pencil
As clever as a cat.

Jenny McDonnell (8)
St John Fisher's RC Primary School, Denton

SNEAKY RATTLESNAKE

The slimy snake is . . .
A sausage pulled and painted,
Put in a pot of grease,
With spiky sandpaper for a tongue.
Slithering through the grass
Waiting for its prey,
Through the overflowing weeds.
The snake is the master of the jungle.

Katie Berry (10)
St John Fisher's RC Primary School, Denton

THE ALLEY CAT

The alley cat is . . .

A one player in its own game,
Eyes of green grass, swaying swiftly in its mind.
Pouncing proudly, but quietly.
Darkly through the dirty city streets.
No fear to the alley cat,
He's king, the city at his feet.

Emma Summerfield (9)
St John Fisher's RC Primary School, Denton

THE DRAGON

The dragon is . . .

An everlasting volcano,
With eyes of burning hot fire.

As she stands tall, the armoured knight
Soaring through the sky, as quiet as a mouse.

The dragon is Vesuvius, the mother of them all.

Elizabeth Summerfield (9)
St John Fisher's RC Primary School, Denton

THE LION KING

The lion is . . .
A furious live teddy bear,
As hard as a shotgun when it's after its prey.
Running rapidly through the African plains
Camouflaged in the grass.
The king of the jungle lies silent in the grass
Waiting to make its next kill.

Jeannette Molloy (10)
St John Fisher's RC Primary School, Denton

THE CROCODILE SNAPPER

The green crocodile is . . .
A nasty jagged saw,
With scales from a safe door,
Silently weaving through the river
Through the river he gets
Closer to his prey
He's the champion murderer of all.

Cory Hallam (10)
St John Fisher's RC Primary School, Denton

THE CHEEKY DOLPHIN

The dolphin is . . .
A shiny diver
With a rubber skin,
Swimming speedily but silently
Through the crystal clear sea.
The dolphin is the child of the sea.

Faye Barcoe (10)
St John Fisher's RC Primary School, Denton

THE ENORMOUS ELEPHANT

There you sit . . .
Buried in the trees
A camouflaged stone boulder
In your stony forest.
You move slowly
Like a giant crane
Walking sideways
Swinging your trunk.

Bryony Wilson (9)
St John Fisher's RC Primary School, Denton

THE PLAYFUL CAT

A cat is a . . .
Big, fluffy, ball of wool
With big, wavy ocean-blue eyes.
The cat plays with butterflies
In the golden corn fields.
The cat is a playful toddler.

Emily Nuttall (10)
St John Fisher's RC Primary School, Denton

THE POUNCING CROCODILE

There you float
In wait for food.
Waiting to pounce.
In your ready camouflage.
You go lick and pounce
Then you go to sleep full up.

Joshua Eccles (9)
St John Fisher's RC Primary School, Denton

SILLY AND SWEET

Down behind the dustbin
I met a dog called Spud -
He was being very silly
Messing in some mud.

Up inside the attic
I met a mouse called O'Malley
He was acting really sweet
Turning all do-lally.

Down behind the dustbin
I met a dog called Sunny.
She was acting very wild chasing
A fluffy bunny.

Up inside the attic
I met a mouse called Molly.
She was acting very horrid
While licking an old lolly.

Ellen Corry (7)
St John Fisher's RC Primary School, Denton

DOG CALLED MOLLY

Down behind the dustbin
I met a dog called Molly
It was raining like mad
So she ran under an old brolly.

Up inside the attic
I met a mouse called Ted
He was snoring so loud
In his tiny little bed.

Down behind the dustbin
I met a dog called Spud.
He fell off the dustbin
And landed with a *thud!*

Catherine Corry (7)
St John Fisher's RC Primary School, Denton

CRAZY ANIMALS

Down behind the dustbin
I met a dog called Peg
She said, 'Go away
Because I'm eating my egg.'

Up inside the attic
I met a mouse called Sam.
He looked so lonely
Nibbling on a piece of ham.

Down behind the dustbin
I met a dog called Molly.
While eating a lolly.

Up inside the attic
I met a dog called Ted.
I saw him jumping
On my old bed.

Jessica Walker (7)
St John Fisher's RC Primary School, Denton

CRAZY ANIMALS

Down behind the dustbin
I met a dog called Molly
She works at a dump
She found a fat dolly.

Up inside the attic
I met a mouse called Sam.
He has a lovely appetite
I said, 'Have a piece of ham!'

Amelia Payne (7)
St John Fisher's RC Primary School, Denton

CRAZY

Up inside the attic
I met a mouse called Molly.
She looked so busy
Eating her ice lolly.

Down behind the dustbin
I met a dog called Sam.
When I looked at him
He was eating a piece of ham.

Up inside the attic
I met a mouse called Kizzy.
When she fell down the hill
She felt really dizzy.

Down behind the dustbin
I met a rat called Ben.
He was running fast
To catch the hen!

Up inside the attic
I met a mouse called Jim.
He was not eating
Because he wanted to be slim.

Kieran Coy (7)
St John Fisher's RC Primary School, Denton

CHEEKY CHAPS

Down behind the dustbin
I met a dog called Spud.
He splashed and splashed
When running in the mud.

Down behind the dustbin
I met a dog called Fang.
She bounced and bounced
And made such a bang.

Down behind the dustbin
I met a dog called Molly.
She said to the baby
'Please may I have your lolly?'

Down behind the dustbin
I met a dog called Pat
'Now is not a good time
Because I'm looking for my rat.'

Shelby Teufel (7)
St John Fisher's RC Primary School, Denton

CRAZY ANIMALS

Down behind the dustbin
I met a dog called Sam.
'It is not a good time now
Because I'm eating ham.'

Up inside the attic
I met a mouse called Kizzy.
When she fell downstairs
She felt very dizzy.

Down behind the dustbin
I met a dog called Meg.
'It is not a good time now
Because I've broken my leg.'

Bethany Robinshaw (7)
St John Fisher's RC Primary School, Denton

GUITAR

Twisting my nose for this harmony,
You see rock stars using me.
Putting a strap from top to bottom,
When they don't use me,
They put me on the bed.
When I break, my strings go *twang*
My electrical socket can go *bang*.
They take me to get repaired
It does not happen
I feel sad
My eyes go droop
My last chance has gone.
I can't help it
I might just cry
They throw me on a dump,
Maybe I'll die.

Sarah-Louise Doyle (10)
St John Fisher's RC Primary School, Denton

Song Of Silence

Silence, silence, begs for you to sleep
So out of mind and thought it will creep.
Round, it dances through toes and fingers,
In your ears its sweet sound lingers.
Excited as a butterfly, calm as a flower,
Gentle and soft as a snowflake shower.
Light as dark, dark as light,
You hear silence, but out of sight.
There's music all around you, yet there is no sound
It's shooting through the sky, burrowing through the ground.

Sophie Summerfield (11)
St John Fisher's RC Primary School, Denton

SHADOW OF THE NIGHT

I get scared as the sun goes down and the moon comes up.
I see a shadow of Wisdom pass by my window every night.
She puts me to sleep making my dreams and ambitions come true.
Tonight I will meet this shadow of kindness
And she will grant me a wish.
She is night
I hear her voice every night.
I see her clothes shining in the moonlight.
I know where she lives
In a mansion under the shadows.
I got my wish to fly,
I flew with Night, her blue and silver cloak with a gold chain
Covers the night to make day.

Bethany Williams (11)
St John Fisher's RC Primary School, Denton

A WALL

I stand there all day,
People graffiti me with spray.
'Ow!' I say as people kick balls at me
Then someone soon comes and sits on my knee.
I stand there blocking the way
But I'm only made of bricks and clay.

Sean Coy (11)
St John Fisher's RC Primary School, Denton

MY OWN NIGHT

My night is kind to me
She covers for me
She gives me big hugs
She makes me so so happy
My night makes me feel safe
She catches all my bad dreams
When she goes I am very sad
But I know my night will be back.

Alice Hibbert (10)
St John Fisher's RC Primary School, Denton

WHAT IS A RAINBOW?

What is a rainbow?
Coloured fairies flying through the sky.
What are snowflakes?
Cut up crackers falling from above.
What is the night sky?
A black silk blanket that has fallen on Earth.
What is thunder?
God playing the drums.

Jennifer Williams (11)
St John Fisher's RC Primary School, Denton

NIGHT

Night is nasty, night is mean
Night will get you, night is keen.
Night is lonely, night is mean,
That's why people are scared of green.
Night is like a spider moving through the woods
And scaring Miss Riding Hood.

Michael McCullion (10)
St John Fisher's RC Primary School, Denton

VEHICLES

Speed, speeding along
The flashy, Suzuki motorbike,
It makes humming *mmmm* sound
It's a dream bike.

Zoom, zooming along
In the sporty Porsche,
It makes *rrrrrr* sound
It's a beauty.

Flash, flashing along
In the red shiny Ferrari!

Sean Pearce (10)
St John's Mosley Common CE Primary School, Worsley

THE WONDERS OF EGYPT

Oh the great Egyptian pyramids towering into the sky,
And the giant staring Sphinx, lifelike to the human eye.

Egypt
Egypt
The wonders of Egypt
What will its treasures reveal?

The mysterious gods of which everyone speaks
With powers much different to you and me.
But if you ever see them you will never believe them
Because the hieroglyphics hold the key.

Egypt
Egypt
The wonders of Egypt
What will its secrets reveal?

But what about the great army of the Egyptians
Race with their speeding chariots with bows
But then you have their driven leader
With a mind that always knows.

But when the sun goes down and everything goes brown,
Just like the wonders of Egypt.

Charlie Thompson (9)
St John's Mosley Common CE Primary School, Worsley

IT'S FUN TO BE AT SCHOOL

School, school it's fun to be there
The teacher's glasses have just gone missing
The teacher has gone looking all over
All the children have their hands up
'Miss they're on your desk' shout the children.

School, school it's fun to be there
The class pens have broken.
The children are all shaking their pens with the tops on.
But the pens' tops have fallen off.
Splat! All over the teacher's face.

School, school, it's fun to be there
5, 4, 3, 2, 1, the bell for play time.
'See you Miss' say the children.
The children jump out of their seats and out of the door.
School, school, it's fun to be there.

Daniel Mottershead (11)
St John's Mosley Common CE Primary School, Worsley

THE FOUR SEASONS

Spring is a new beginning.
Spring means flowers start budding.
Spring is the joy of baby lambs.
Spring means leaves are growing back.

Winter is time to build snowmen
Winter is time to wrap up warm.
Winter is there to have fun.
Winter is time to skate all around.

When summer comes it's time to go out.
Summer's here you need water for plants.
When summer's here you sit in pools of water.
Summer's here you hear children playing.

Autumn is a time when the flowers die
Autumn is a time when the leaves fall off trees.
Autumn is a time when different colours come
Autumn is a time when the animals collect berries.

Sarah Hart (9)
St John's Mosley Common CE Primary School, Worsley

THE LIFE OF A RIVER

The life of a river starts off as a stream
It trickles over the stones
It flows gently all the way as you may have seen.

Until it reaches the end of the stream
The end of the stream is a tiny waterfall
It bubbles over the rocks as you may have seen.

After the waterfall at the stream
The stream turns into a river
It whooshes along as you may have seen.

Until it reaches the end of the river
The waterfall at the end
It *crashes* down and sprays as it hits the rocks
If you were there it would make you shiver!

Zoë Gibson (10)
St John's Mosley Common CE Primary School, Worsley

MY DOG

My dog
A happy dog
Always playful, full of fun spots

My dog
A spotty dog
With three black spots

My dog
A small dog
With a long bushy tail

My dog
A spotty dog
With three black spots

My dog
A black and white dog
With four white paws

My dog
A spotty dog
With three black spots

My dog
A floppy dog
With big brown eyes

My dog
A spotty dog
With three black spots

My dog
A sharp dog
With four little legs.

My dog
A spotty dog
With three black spots.

My dog
A happy dog
Always playful with me.

Ashley Croker (10)
St John's Mosley Common CE Primary School, Worsley

DOGS

Dogs, dogs, large, small, fat or thin tails
They wag them when glad.
Dogs, dogs don't like cat's wails
They chase them when mad.

Dogs, dogs always bark.
They are playful too.
Dogs, dogs like going to play at a park
They like to play with you.

Dogs, dogs all have a name
Like Jasper, Kaiser.
Dogs, dogs like to play games
Some dogs are wiser.

Dogs, dogs have good speeds
Some dogs eat bones.
Dogs, dogs have needs.
Some have high tones.

William Hayes (10)
St John's Mosley Common CE Primary School, Worsley

CAMERON MY BROTHER

Blue, blue, blue for a boy,
Blue is for the sky,
And my brother's toys.
Blue for his jumper,
And his blue remote control car.

Blue is for his favourite band
His nicest drink is blue bubblegum flavour
Blue for his sparkling eyes
And his room is also blue
Blue is for his books.

Blue is for his toothbrush
And his blue fancy crayons,
My brother has nearly everything *blue*
Blue, blue, blue, blue,
Blue, blue, blue, blue.

My brother's favourite colour.

Chelsea Renshaw (9)
St John's Mosley Common CE Primary School, Worsley

THE SEA

Shells and pebbles being washed away by the splashing of the waves.
Dolphins squeaking as they play.
Splashing sounds as children play in the water.
Seagulls singing as they fly so very high in the sky.
People walking up and down the plankton hearing footsteps
                                    as they walk.
Dogs barking on the beach
People flickering water with their feet.

Sharelle Robinson (9)
St John's Mosley Common CE Primary School, Worsley

THIS CRAZY WORLD

Here within this crazy world where things are not
as they should be.

Birds chirping, music playing
They swap their sound
People singing, people swaying
That is something that I've found.

Very slow minutes and very fast hours
People wonder why
In this crazy world we have water-squirting flowers
Also there are birds that cannot fly.

The sun, it shines at night
The moon comes out in the day
It gives me quite a fright
So I watch, then walk away.

The snow it falls in July
Hot sun you feel in December
When the sun goes I feel so shy
When the white snow comes
I know it is a time to remember.

Please, help me through this crazy world
I don't know where I am.

Shannon Tiernan (9)
St John's Mosley Common CE Primary School, Worsley

My Bedroom

In my bedroom I put my tapes on
I play my games.

In my bedroom I get my clothes out of my wardrobe
And get dressed so I can play with my Lego.

In my bedroom I feed my fish
Then I have my food in a dish.

In my bedroom I switch on my reading lamp
And start reading.

In my bedroom I shut my blind
Then I try to see what I can find.

In my bedroom I turn on my TV
And then I listen to my favourite CD.

When I hurt myself I run to my room,
Lock my door and look at the clock.

Finally when it is my bedtime, I go to bed.

Michael Norbury (8)
St John's Mosley Common CE Primary School, Worsley

THE SKY

The night sky shimmers with gleaming stars
Under the moonlight sky.
As the night passes over
The moon tucks away,
For the day, as the children laugh and play
Under the scorching sun.
Then comes dinner
As the sun shimmers
Later on in the midday sun the children are
Playing under the fluffy clouds.
Bedtime comes, the children
Are no longer playing under the sun.
The sun fades away as the moon
Gives a shine in
The sky!

Daniel Winnard (9)
St John's Mosley Common CE Primary School, Worsley

THE SKY

White snow falling down onto the rocky ground
The sun comes out to melt away the snow.
At night it's starry
In the morning it is fluffy
When it's winter it is windy.

Heather Sharples (9)
St John's Mosley Common CE Primary School, Worsley

AUTUMN

Autumn comes
When summer goes
The wind pushes the leaves
When it blows.
Leaves fall to the ground
Without a sound
Collect the leaves when
They fall from the trees.
The leaves flow and the
Colours 'glow.'
I love autumn
I wish it wouldn't
Go!

Sophie Mason (8)
St John's Mosley Common CE Primary School, Worsley

ART

A rt is great
R ed paint is nice
T he paints are all different colours

Carly Newton (7)
St Mary's RC Primary School, Failsworth

SWIMMING

S   wimming is cool! To be in the pool

W ell I just love swimming, yes I do

I   t is not boring at all

M e and my friend love it

M y mum says she can't swim but I know she can

I   n the water the bodies go

N ow it's time I've got to go

G osh! I had a great time.

Olivia Prescott (8)
St Mary's RC Primary School, Failsworth

SWIMMING

S   wimming is great
W e get lots of exercise
I   n the pool we get very wet
M y friend is good
M y friend is called Eleanor
I   n the pool we work hard
N ow I swim like a fish like Eleanor
G o swimming, it's great exercise!

Chantelle Martin (8)
St Mary's RC Primary School, Failsworth

ART

A rt is great to do
R eally I love art
T he art lesson is good.

Natasha Lees (8)
St Mary's RC Primary School, Failsworth

HISTORY

H istory is perfect
I t tells you stuff about the past
S tories about history are in some shops
T udors ate live creatures for dinner
O ld coins are in some museums
R omans had arenas to see gladiators
Y ou can read books about history.

Luke Joyce (8)
St Mary's RC Primary School, Failsworth

ART

A   rt is great, art is good
R   eally it is my favourite
T   he things we do are great in art.

Alison Clarke (8)
St Mary's RC Primary School, Failsworth

ART IS GREAT

A rt is great and the
R ight thing for me
T he teachers are great.
    Art is great. I love it yes!

Eleanor Rowan (8)
St Mary's RC Primary School, Failsworth